SISTERS IGNITED MEDIA & PUBLISHING INC.

Edited by Sisters Ignited Media & Publishing Inc.

Cover art by Rachelle Van Ryssen

 Sisters Ignited Media   Layout by Sisters Ignited Media & Publishing Inc.

Printed by permission.

Sisters Ignited Media & Publishing Inc.

Simcoe, Ontario, Canada

PublisherWebsite.com https://simpinc.info/

Know Stress No Stress!

By Albert J. Varga

Dedication

This book is dedicated to all those who are recovering or have recovered from addiction, anxiety/ panic attacks, cancer survivors, victims of PTSD and other stress disorders. Finally, I would like to thank my wife Judith Hill for her support and compassion to myself and others.

Contents

Know Stress No Stress!

About the Author

Albert Jonathan Varga is a retired stress management consultant from Burlington, Ontario, Canada. Mr. Varga runs a free, online crisis counselling service called Lifenet Crisis Counselling Services Inc. Lifenet counsellors are volunteer professionals who hold degrees in addictions, psychology, or social work. Clients who access Lifenet services present with a vast array of social history including veterans, cancer survivors, LGBT (lesbian, gay, bisexual, transgender) assault victims, Post Traumatic Stress Disorder (PTSD), Obsessive-Compulsive Disorder (OCD), and cult survivors.

Mr. Varga has conducted seminars for many prestigious companies including, Folk Garten International, Health Sense, and Chamber of Commerce. Information contained in this book is not a replacement for a physicians' or other health care practitioners' care.

Introduction

Are you stressed? If you know what causes stress—if you know all about the illusions, it projects—you are no longer stressed. This book proposes stratagem behind the illusion stress causes and presents therapeutic tools for re-anchoring emotional and cognitive experiences linked to illusory stressors.

Stress management tips include eating well, managing stress in the workplace and other time-honoured solutions. These tips will start you on your journey to living a stress-free life. Is that possible? Yes. Stressful situations will always be around; managing stress determines our ability to engage in a stress-free life.

Intended Learning Objectives Include:

1. A thought is just a thought.

2. Entertainment of a thought causes stress, or freedom from stress.

Counselling sessions contained in this book are condensed for enlightenment and learning purposes only. Any client that seems familiar to you is strictly coincidental.

Chapter 1

Stress Management the Easy Way

Research has demonstrated that your body will respond to your brains' instruction. The next time you feel stressed over a situation in your life, try dancing and singing about it. You will notice that changing a default response to stressors will cause decreased stressful feelings about the situation.

Typical responses to stress relief include people engaging in alcohol consumption and other substances, smoking, or comfort food—none of these responses to stress matter because stress is BS. BS is an acronym for 'baloney sandwich.' So, metaphorically speaking, stress is baloney sandwiched between your brain and your imagination. If you are experiencing anxiety, panic attacks, phobias, OCD, stress in the workplace, stress at home, and stress in relationships— nothing more than baloney sandwiches.

Know Stress No Stress!

Therapeutic techniques presented in the following pages may temporarily relieve readers from their symptoms.

At times people have approached me and said, "Hey Albert, do you have any quick tips for stress?"

"Absolutely. Eat as much junk food as you like, don't get a lick of exercise, don't drink any water, don't get any sleep, and worry as much as you can."

"No, Albert, we meant tips for stress management, not stress." "That's different. Eat a well-balanced nutritious diet, exercise, drink plenty of water, get plenty of sleep, and don't worry."

Five Common Sense Tips:

When stressed, you would be surprised how many people will not follow common sense.

1. ## Monitor your diet.

    a. When stressed, people often turn to comfort food for temporary relief. Comfort foods often contain large amounts of sugar and saturated fats. High blood sugar and fat content aggravate stress levels, which causes stress on the heart and can increase the risk for heart disease.

2. ## Exercise for thirty minutes a day.

    a. Thirty minutes of exercise can be broken down into ten-minute intervals.

3. ## Maintain seven to eight hours of sleep per night.

    a. Some people can survive on six hours of sleep per night.

    b. According to medical experts, people who have trouble sleeping because of chronic pain will sleep for 4 hours per night and nap for two hours per day, which is fine.

4. Worry less.

    a. The more you worry, the more you create neural pathways that signal worry in your brain. Your brain signals are caught in one endless loop, and minor stressors in your life magnify into one colossal stressor.

5. Try meditation.

    a. Meditation can take many forms.

    b. There are no set rules for meditation.

    c. Simple observation is an excellent form of meditation.

        i. You can observe beaches, therapeutic massage, your wedding, or family photo albums.

    d. Thirty minutes of meditation is equivalent to two hours of sleep.

Some people deal with their stress through various forms of art; drawing, painting, or attending art exhibitions. Other people relieve stress by showing generosity; reporting they glean a wonderful intrinsic feeling and enjoy their day by giving of themselves. Others stop and consider alternative activities that would be less stressful on their mind and body. Some people deal with stress by reading their favourite books, including comic books.

Physical touch, such as hugging and cuddling your significant other or best friend, is another excellent stress reliever. Some people turn to sports to relieve stress--whether watching or participating.

I, personally, like all sports--hockey, football, soccer, basketball, baseball, volleyball, tennis, badminton, golf, and pool. Born and raised in Hamilton, Ontario, I became a Tiger Cat fan. My friend, however, believes the Tiger-Cats are aging and alleges they lose every year. My friends' perspective denotes a common characteristic of people experiencing stress--they choose to view situations from a negative versus a positive lens.

The Tiger-Cats won the grey cup fifteen times and are likely to win many more. My friend says his favourite hockey team is the Toronto Maple Leaf's; however, sometimes he compares them with the Titanic, alleging they both look great until they hit the ice. From a positive perspective, one can note that the Toronto Maple Leaf's won the Stanley Cup more than 15 times.

My friend says he likes hockey, but it is not his favourite sport because he is not into violent sports. His favourite sport is kickboxing. He says the reason for this is because the goal of kickboxing is to beat each other up, the goal of hockey is to get the puck from one end to the other and score the puck in the net, not to beat each other up.

Golf is a great way to relieve stress, although I sometimes don't understand the attraction of repeatedly hitting the ball in a hole. Some holes I find more difficult than others, especially when trying to hit the ball past a tiny windmill that keeps bouncing the ball back to me. Despite the occasional challenge, I find the repetitive engagement in golf a trite boring.

My favourite sport is the game of pool. Playing pool presents striking similarities to golf without the possibility of getting a hernia or a sunburn.

By now, your brain has been giving you various images. When you envisioned hockey players, what colour were their uniforms? What colour were their shirts? Did one of them have a beard? Were the kickboxers fighting in a ring or a cage? Did you visualize the titanic lighting up at night with all its colours? Did you capture an image of the little windmill bouncing the ball back to me? What colour was it?

It is important to note that I didn't give you the details of those events, but your brain provided you with creative images. This exercise is known as filling in. Without more information, the brain will search your memory for something to compare it to and often presents a pleasant scenario for you to enjoy. Unfortunately, this exercise can have the opposite effect. When experiencing stress or a stressful event in your life, the brain will search your memory for something to compare it to and often presents a frightening scenario or a solution based on addictive behaviour.

We have all been duped, stressed, and deceived by our brains. We have been lied to, told half-truths—similar to election time. And all for nothing because your brain has created images and stories that are not real. Is it possible that you engage in an addictive habit because your brain says it makes you happy when experiencing stress? Yet, that is not the case. We

Know Stress No Stress!

are inundated with images every day. Why not bombard yourself with relaxing images?

Chapter 2

The Brain and Stress

To understand how the brain works, we need to examine the brain. It may interest you that the brain is primarily composed of fat tissue. If you looked at a picture of the brain, it would resemble a bowl of leftover perogies your mother used to put in the fridge.

Understand How the Brain Reacts to Stress— Four Areas of the Brain:

1. Occipital Lobe: Do you remember being told in science class that the occipital lobe is located in the back of the brain and controls vision? Oddly, I would have put it in front of the brain, closer to the eyes.

2. Temporal Lobes: Temporal lobes are located beside the temples. This area of the brain controls hearing and forms of communication like language and speech.

3. Frontal Lobes: Frontal lobes are located in the front of the brain and are considered our behaviour and emotional control centre. Creativity is prevalent on the right side and logic on the left.

4. Amygdala: The amygdala sits on the top, left side of the brain. The amygdala is responsible for controlling memories--pleasant or otherwise.

When you experience stressors or an adverse event in your life, your brain signals are caught in one endless loop in the emotional part of your brain. Breaking the loop is as simple as learning how to redistribute brain signals. How do you do that?

One technique is to imagine a golden ray of light descending upon your head and filling your brain with warmth and brightness. Next, imagine red erasers going into the amygdala and erasing your negative/ stressful thoughts. Presto! There are no more negative thoughts, anxiety, panic attacks, phobias, or obsessive, compulsive behaviours.

"Come on, Albert; it can't be that simple? That sounds a little juvenile, silly, and ridiculous."

"That may be true, but doesn't it also sounds a little juvenile, silly, and ridiculous when you have a stressful thought or experience obsessive-compulsive behaviours? Doesn't it feel silly when you experience a phobia, panic attack, or anxiety?" The brain does not know the difference between thoughts based on reality and fantasy. The brain takes everything you say literally.

The brain can only focus on one thing at a time while scanning six others. Based on fantasy, we have 70,000 thoughts per day, which equals 46 thoughts per minute. We need to create three positive images to replace every negative image created in our minds.

If remembering past adverse events can be experienced as a reality in the present moment, can we apply the same process to remembering pleasant events? Next time you go to the beauty salon to get your hair done, have a manicure, pedicure, or even a Swedish massage, notice how wonderful it feels. Be aware of the endorphins (pleasure effect) you experience. Once you experience the endorphins, form a circle with your index finger and thumb, and soak up those feel-good hormones.

You can apply the same process the next time you are experiencing stress.

Form a circle with the same index finger and thumb and share the same endorphins. It works for about a minute or two. Your brain remembers your relaxed state of mind when you form the circle. This process is known as an association.

Similarly, a past negative experience may be associated with a song on the radio. In the present moment, hearing the same music causes the brain to associate the past negative experience with the theme. Suddenly you experience an anxiety attack without knowing why--until now.

Practical Exercise:

1. Think of a subject that causes you to experience negative thoughts.

2. Think of positive thoughts to contradict the negative.

3. Write your ideas down on paper.

4. Make two columns. One column lists your negative thoughts, and the other list your positive thoughts.

I am irrational and illogical.	I am rational and logical.
I struggle to reach my goals.	I will easily reach my goals.
People don't like me. I have to pretend to be someone I am not.	People like me for who I am. I don't have to pretend to be someone I am not.
I cannot control my thoughts.	I am in control of my thoughts.
Nobody likes me. Nobody loves	I am well-liked and loved.
I can't do anything right. I always make mistakes.	Errors are not errors; they are discoveries of how things don't work.

The Brain and Neurotransmitters:

To attain increased energy, motivation, and a feeling of well-being, stimulate the brain's four neurotransmitters—dopamine, acetylcholine, gamma-aminobutyric acid (GABA), and serotonin.

Foods that Increase Neurotransmitter Levels in the Brain:

1. Dopamine
    a. Meat and dairy products
2. Acetylcholine
    a. Eggs, fish, blueberries, and peanut butter
3. GABA
    a. Bananas, broccoli, and brown rice
4. Serotonin
    a. Avocados, poultry, and wheat germ

Sensory Experience:

Stimulate the olfactory sensors with lavender if you need to elevate your mood but are on a diet. The odor releases serotonin giving you a feeling of well-being. If lavender isn't your favourite scent, meditate on a peaceful scene containing green colours. In as little as three minutes, you will experience a reduction in your heart rate and blood pressure. A feeling of well-being will permeate your being.

Visualization is key to stress management. Is it difficult? It is no more difficult than visualizing failure, a horrifying future, a past adverse event, or making up negative stories and scenarios in your mind. Visualization involves maintaining a relaxed state of mind. Pay attention to the suggestions you make in positive visualizations. Do not become critical or logical about the visualizations. Avoid contradictory thoughts such as, "The visualizations can't possibly be true." "With all the stress you are experiencing, you can't possibly feel relaxed."

Practical Exercise:

Finding a place free from interruption or noise is essential when you implement positive visualizations. NOTE: Practicing visualization techniques while operating a motor vehicle or heavy equipment is not advisable.

1. Sit slightly recline but not flat, close your eyes and relax.

2. Imagine waves of relaxation slowly descending onto your body from your head downwards; imagine the waves breaking up the stress.

3. The waves move down over your head, to your neck, torso, arms, and legs.

4. Feel everything in your body relaxing as the waves of relaxation envelop you.

5. If that visual doesn't resonate with you, try focusing your eyes on an object in the room.

6. Or visualize stepping into a secure elevator with a magnificent view of the mountains. As the elevator slowly descends toward land, you feel an increased sense of relaxation.

7. The method used is irrelevant as long as it is relaxing and non-threatening.

8. Once you are in your quiet place, repeat to yourself, "I am relaxed." "I am Calm."

9. You can choose to implement positive visualizations to manage and reduce stress.

Meditation Techniques:

Meditation is a valuable technique. You can relax your body and clear your head of stressful thoughts. The method behind meditation is a simple one--focus your thoughts, on one object, or pleasant scene. As mentioned, your brain can only focus on one thing at a time while scanning six others. During meditation, we focus on something that relaxes us— practicing for twenty minutes to start—frequent practice results in less time required to experience deep relaxation.

You may want to add a mantra (so to speak) to your meditation practice. Many people prefer the classic Sanskrit word, 'Om,' which translates into the English word 'perfection.' If you are a Christian, you may focus on Jesus. Regardless of the technique you use it is crucial to stay focused.

If other thoughts distract you, imagine them inside a balloon, drifting out of sight. The use of imagery is an effective way to reduce stress. You already use it when you imagine adverse events and misinterpret things in your mind's eye.

Do you remember your relaxing trip to the Caribbean, Mexico, Barbados, and Florida? Why not use your imagination to recreate the memory as if you were still there? The more pleasant and pictorial you imagine this place, the more realistic it will become for the brain. Remember, the brain doesn't know the difference between thoughts based on reality and fantasy.

Your brain is a mass of nerve cells and brain signals. Your sensory parietal lobe transfers signals from your thoughts into electromagnetic impulses. These impulses travel to the part of your brain responsible for visualization and memory; your pictorial images and memories can become real--as if you were still there.

Finger Meditation Technique:

This technique can be done without the knowledge of anyone in the room.

1. Place your thumb on your index finger and think of a beautiful experience.

2. Place your thumb on your middle finger and think of a loving, warm experience.

3. Place your thumb on your fourth finger and think of the best compliment anyone has given you.

4. Place your thumb on your baby finger and remember the most beautiful place you have ever visited or would like to see.

Positive Affirmations:

Repeat the following affirmations to yourself or write them on index cards for easy reference.

1. I let go of tension.
2. I dissolve tension away.
3. I am feeling calm and relaxed.
4. I relax at will.
5. I am in harmony with my life.
6. My thoughts turn inward, and I am at ease.
7. I visualize myself as relaxed, comfortable, and still.
8. I feel an inward quietness.
9. I am peaceful, calm, and serene.
10. I turn stress down like the volume on a radio.
11. I look inward and find peace.

Sleep Hygiene Tips:

Most people need between six and eight hours of sleep per night. On occasion, sleeping four or five hours per night is not a big deal. Perhaps it is all your body needs at that time.

To fall asleep faster:

1. Wake up at the same time each morning, including weekends.

2. Avoid bright light before retiring.
3. Have a candle-lit bath.

4. Read a book with lighting from a small lamp.

5. Do not engage in stressful activities before bedtime, such as paying bills or playing exciting games.

6. Place lavender or jasmine scents near your pillow when you sleep. These two fragrances are said to stimulate the olfactory sensors and induce a state of relaxation.

7. Exercise is essential to assuring a good night's sleep, provided it is done at least three hours before retiring. Your body temperature elevates during exercise, and

ample time is required for your body temperature to cool down.

8. Eat a light snack at bedtime that contains tryptophan-turkey, milk, cheese, or peanut butter.

9. Avoid drinking alcohol at night.

10. Change sleeping position and avoid spicy foods as well as chocolate and coffee.

11. Avoid heavy meals three hours before bedtime.

12. Avoid lying down after eating.

Happiness:

Research suggests that happiness can improve physical health in various capacities, including cardiovascular health, immune health, decreased inflammation levels, and blood pressure. Happiness may extend ones' lifespan and offer a sense of well-being. Enough about what pleasure can do. How do you acquire satisfaction?

There is a difference between what we think will make us happy and what makes us happy. People often believe that happiness will come when they reach an unrealistic goal. This assumption presents a vicious cycle in that they achieve their goal and are happy for a while; then experience boredom and commence to seek another goal in hopes of evading boredom.

I've heard it all, "I will finally be happy when I am rich and famous. I will be happy when I meet the girl of my dreams. I will be happy when I get a good-paying job." People don't live in the present; they live for the future. I live in the present because the past can offer me nothing, and the future is uncertain. The present is a gift of happiness.

Insightful Quotes from the Expert's:

1. Happiness is letting go of what you think your life is supposed to look like. ~ Unknown

2. A key to happiness is knowing you have the power to choose what to accept and what to let go of. ~ Dodinsky

3. Happiness is not something ready-made. It comes from your actions. ~ Dalai Lama

4. There is no path to happiness. Happiness IS the path. ~ Buddha

5. Happiness is a direction, not a place. ~ Sydney L. Harris

6. Be happy for no reason, like a child. ~ Deepak Chopra

7. Choose to be happy, that is the only way to find happiness. ~ Debases Mridha

8. No one can make you happy until you are satisfied with yourself first. ~ Unknown

9. The only thing that will make you happy is being happy with who you are. ~ Goldie Hawn

10. Happiness is a choice, not a result. Nothing will make you happy until you choose to be satisfied. ~ Ralph Marston

11. Happiness is not out there; it's in you. ~ Unknown

12. Happiness is a choice, not a result. Nothing will make you happy until you choose to be satisfied. ~ Unknown

13. If you want others to be happy, practice compassion. If you want to be happy, practice compassion. ~ Dalai Lama

14. Very little is needed to make a happy life; it is all within yourself, in your way of thinking. ~ Marcus Aurelius Antoninus

15. Happiness is a habit. Cultivate it. ~ Elbert Hubbard

16. In your journey to happiness, take a break and just be happy. ~ Albert Varga

17. You're only as happy and free as you think you are. ~ Albert Varga

18. People are just as happy as they make their minds up to be. ~ Abraham Lincoln

19. Happiness is mindfulness. That is, not regretting the past, not worrying about the future, but enjoying the present moment. ~ Albert Varga

Here is the bottom line. Do you want to be happy? How can you be happy? Talking and acting as if you are already delighted can trigger your subconscious into believing you are happy.

Leisure activities like watching a movie or cuddling with a significant other can create instant happiness. Physical activities such as walking, and strength training can induce a happy, confident state of mind. Eating healthy has a considerable effect on the brain—feel healthy and feel good. Happiness is intrinsic—a state of being versus doing. Being miserable, however, takes work.

Stress Management 101:

1. An excellent way to relax and boost your mood is to increase body temperature. Exercise, a warm bath, or shower will increase body temperature and produce endorphins. Did you know you could also receive the same effect by simply visualizing yourself in a hot bath or lying on a warm sandy beach? Picture the scene in your mind, and mentally repeat the phrase, "I am warm and relaxed."

2. Refuse to let anyone rob you of peace and contentment. Some people will intentionally try to offend you to get a reaction. Instead, choose to walk away or compliment them. That will drive them crazy.

3. Set realistic goals or expectations for yourself and others. You may find yourself feeling disappointed or depressed. Try to do the best you can and forget about it. If others don't meet your expectations, it's not their problem; it's yours. They have set their own goals.

4. You can relieve stress by interacting with like-minded people. We need contact with others. Engaging in worship, team sports, or dinner with a special friend lowers blood pressure.

5. Got stress? Journal both the stressor and the solution. Use the journal entries as a training manual for future issues.

6. The pessimist says the glass is half empty; the optimist says it's half full. If you tend to be a pessimist, you may unconsciously attribute negative interpretations to everyday events. Focus on the optimistic, positive interpretations and watch your mood change.

7. If your spouse plans a night out, plan a fun activity for yourself.

8. Want to relieve stress? Getting fresh air in the great outdoors is just what the doctor ordered.

9. Got stress? Thoughts of pleasurable events will reduce stress.

10. Three words that cause stress: would've, should've, could've. These words pass judgment on yourself and

others and can cause feelings of guilt. Simple solution—STOP!!!

11. Experience boredom quickly? Plan multiple, light activities. Ditch the self-defeating attitude.

12. Everyone has down days—even me. Don't beat yourself up if you feel stressed. Cheer up and put on a happy face.

13. Stressed by a problem? It's easy to get emotional and make decisions you'll regret later. Relax and meditate, then return to the problem with a peaceful approach.

14. Stressed? Rushed? Anxious? Take a moment to examine your surroundings. Be aware of all your senses, and then zero in on the real problem.

15. It's nice to plan for the future, but don't forget the present.

16. If a futuristic, negative scenarios play in your mind tell yourself you will deal with it when the time comes—if it comes.

17. Sometimes, things happen because they happen. Adjust your focus to something you can directly affect.

18. Do you ever think about negative things from the past and re-live the stress? Focus on where you are going, not where you have been. Looking behind you produces neck pain.

    a. Philippians 3:13 NIV Brothers and sisters, I do not consider myself yet to have taken hold of it. But one thing I do: Forgetting what is behind and straining toward what is ahead.

19. Stuck in a dead-end job? Stressed because you are stuck in university for four years, and this is only your second year? Are thinking about your future and painting a false picture? Paint a positive scene and accept that you are exactly where you need to be to prepare for a better future. Consider it training.

20. Worrying about the future creates negative behavioural patterns and amplifies trivial stressors. Learning to deal with minor stressors allows the brain opportunities to practice healthy stress management techniques.

21. Be happy with what you have. Count your blessings.

22. Focus on what you are doing in the present. If a negative thought arises, tell yourself you'll get back to it later. It is probably irrelevant and won't come back if it is negative.

23. If, at first, you don't succeed, keep trying. Wrong! If, at first, you don't succeed, try something different.

24. Avoid the word try. Saying, "I will try to relax," causes the brain to interpret your words literally and applies the message to your body. 'Sounds great, just let me know when you want to relax.'

25. Do this, don't do that, can't you read the sign? We are programmed to do what is right. What is right is not always authentic but rather the status quo. Is it worth the pressure trying to please others? Choose to say no to people who ask you to do things that don't line up with your values.

26. When faced with a stressful event, see yourself as a stress management guru. How will you manage the stressful event?

27. Want to be free from anxiety, fear, and stress? Visualize yourself as the kung fu master of tension. Face your

nonsensical fears and visualize yourself kicking the Jimin crickets out of them.

28. Do you have negative scenarios coming to your mind when you least expect them? Erase them, literally. Picture yourself with a huge eraser—rub the picture off the page of your mind.

29. Stressed people solve their problems by ritualistically pouring a drink, having a cigarette, or eating a chocolate bar. Why not get ritualistic about taking a bath, listening to soothing music, changing into comfortable clothing.

30. Take a break from the routine. If you go to church in a suit and tie, dress more casually. If you eat raisin bran cereal every morning, try a bran muffin. Give the brain some variety; if you stick to a routine, the brain signals may stick to a pattern of acting in a stressful manner.

31. If you have a task to complete and you are too stressed to do it, offer yourself a reward. You can also take breaks at various intervals throughout the task.

32. Have a fun weekend. Cheat on your diet occasionally (but just a bit). Designate one day a week for pizza day, movie day, or mini golf.

33. Avoid critical people. Ignore those who seek to make you angry. Refuse to attend pity parties. Don't let others mold you into their way of thinking. You are your own person.

34. Do you want to reduce stress levels? Research common stressors and associated triggers. Observe how people manage positive or negative stress.

35. Don't do anything I wouldn't do—wrong advice. Instead consider Dr. Ruth's advice, "If it feels good—do it!"

36. Put on a happy face, even when you are stressed. If you maintain that joker smile for five minutes, your stress may disappear. Dance and sing about the stress.

37. If people see you stressed, it may be easy for them to manipulate you. Don't invite others to use you. Talk to someone you trust. Smile and remain silent until you can get to a counsellor.

38. Exercise is a great stress reducer and sometimes eliminator. Instead of stressing over the task at hand, think of ways to make exercise fun.

39. On a scale of 1-10, how bad can the situation be? Ten would be swimming with sharks and forgetting your

bathing suit; one would be running out of bran flakes. Now, how awful is the situation?

40. Journal stressful situations and techniques used to manage or avoid the situations. The journal will provide possible solutions moving forward.

41. Eliminate stress by getting back to a simple life. Read, walk, volunteer, have a slumber party, take pictures—do anything easy and fun.

42. Energize the intellectual side of your brain by reading, doing puzzles, playing chess, or playing board games.

43. For a guaranteed quick fix, an instant stress reliever, walk through a garden or greenhouse rich in plants. Plants take in carbon dioxide and give off oxygen.

44. Say no to sugar, and you will say no to stress. Chemicals like sugar, caffeine, and MSG can cause depression, anger, anxiety, panic attacks, and general feelings of inky stinky.

45. Spend time with happy people; you will find it contagious.

46. Change or add to your routine. If you listen to classical music, add jazz music. If you go for a walk every night,

take a different route. Only go out on weekends, try a weeknight?

47. Exercise both mentally and physically. Try reading while on the stationary bike. Although watching tv is not as beneficial, it will stimulate the brain, and take your mind off exercising.

Everyone feels depressed at one time or another. We can choose to dwell on the negative inner voice that tells us there are no solutions, or we can listen to the cheerful inner voice that tells us there is a way out of our negative feelings. Positive action is easily engaged when you know how.

Two general rules:

1. Examine and communicate your negative feelings and depressed thoughts.

2. Create a plan of action and follow through with it.

Plan of Action:

1. Write your feelings in a book. When you write down your feelings, they appear more concrete and therefore more difficult to avoid. You can analyze your written feelings saying to yourself, "Are things that bad?" "What steps can I take to avoid these feelings?" Remember you are the director and the controller of your thoughts. What you think determines what you feel. Your brain and heart will follow your instruction. Writing your thoughts on paper is a form of relief. Self-expression may feel difficult because we fear what others think. Are you mad at someone, and you can't share your feelings? Express yourself in written form. Relieve your frustrations through a pen. If you have negative thoughts about your self-worth, yell at yourself on paper. "Negative thoughts out now! You're useless to me! I'm in charge! I'm in control!" Allow positive thoughts and creative ideas to flow through you.

2. Exercise. Take a walk, go swimming, and move your energy. Exercise will temporarily refocus your thoughts and

release endorphins in your body. Feeling more refreshed, you can deal with your thoughts in a positive manner.

3. Confide in someone you trust. If you feel you can't trust anyone; connect with one of our free counsellors. Don't let things bottle up inside.

4. Help others. Get involved in a community project. Do something good for someone in need. When we are focused on others, our problems may not look as bad.

5. Take a break. Soak in a bathtub, go to a movie or rent a funny video. Laughter is good medicine. Don't ignore your problems, but don't let problems consume you. There is an answer to every problem, and tomorrow is another day. If you have experienced a loss (death in the family, loss of employment, relationship break-up), depressed feelings are normal. The feeling of grief will pass. Again, if you feel you can't cope, seek out a counsellor.

Chapter 3

Counselling Sessions

The following sessions are fictional in nature but are based on my work as a therapist. Sessions are condensed to protect the innocent and the guilty. These sessions should assist the reader in reducing stress-related disorders by following the various stress management tools presented. Each case is individual and may not apply to every reader.

Session One:

My office was dimly lit; a soothing glow from the lights above emitted a relaxed, tranquil aura. The soft Corinthian leather sofa and my chair completed an atmosphere of comfort and safety for clients. I'm a stress management therapist dealing with individuals who struggle with anxiety, panic attacks, PTSD, addiction, and OCD.

I sat at my desk waiting for my first client of the day who reported he suffered from a litany of stress-related disorders. I use past tense when referencing a client's experience because their symptoms are often greatly reduced upon completion of a therapy session. Exceptions are mental illnesses requiring medication; clients may experience a reduction in symptoms but still require medication. Before an appointment, I always insist clients speak with their physician prior to discontinuing any medication.

A startling buzz came from my intercom, making me jump.

"Mr. Varga, your nine o'clock has arrived."

"Thank you, Audrey; please show him in."

From the onset of her job interview, I knew Audrey was a suitable candidate. She was warm, compassionate, maternal, meticulous, and efficient. Plus, she was the only one that submitted a resume for the position.

Audrey always dressed professional and had a pleasant demeanor. Today was no exception as she ushered in Mr. Rogers and offered him a seat on the sofa. I rose from my desk chair and smiled so intensely one would have thought I won the lottery.

"Welcome, Mr. Rogers. What's on your mind that you would like to change today?"

Then I sat down. This introductory question catches everyone off guard. The question sets the stage for their unconscious change work.

His smile changed to a frown.

"Well, I um I have PTSD," he said to my tie.

"Look at me when you're speaking to me, not at my tie."

That threw him off guard. Did he remember being talked

to like that by a parent, teacher, or drill sergeant? This time my smile was slight, paternal, and warm, which again it threw him off guard as he was expecting the look of a military general.

"Sorry sir," he said.

He looked right at me but did not present signs of fearfulness.

"No problem. It's common for clients to avoid eye contact during the onset of our conversations. It also means your brain is functioning normally."

"Now, let's cut to the chase. How long have you been living with PTSD, and what division did you serve with?"

"Division? Oh, no, wait, I was never in the military. My PTSD resulted from three scary events that happened all in the same year."

"I'm listening."

This time he spoke to his shoes.

"That year, I had a strangulated hernia and required surgery. I had an allergic reaction to Valium, and I struggled to breathe.

(as he shared, his breathing became a struggle).

During that same year, I was in a plane crash. A few months later, I experienced anxiety, and panic attacks. I started drinking more, eating junk food, and struggled with OCD."

"Perfect," I said. "I'm happy to hear that."

He looked up in disbelief. Did he think I was mocking him?

"Why are you happy to hear that?"

As if to say, "You're a cruel sadist!"

"I am happy to hear that because after traumatic events it is normal to experience stress-related reactions. So once again, your brain is working normally."

He scratched an imaginary itch in his ear.

"So, what do I do about it? Will this go away? Will I ever get better? Will I ever get a decent sleep?"

"Yes, to all three. It is likely that you will feel better before you walk out of this office this morning. Well, except for the sleep. You have to do that at home as I have another client coming at 10:30 am."

"You're funny," he laughed and then smiled.

"Oh, caught you laughing and smiling."
"That you did."

Taking a deep breath, he sat back on the couch.

"So now what?"

"Now we order coffee." Again, he smiled.

"You're cool."

"Thanks," I said as I returned the smile and made my way to the intercom.

"Hey there, Audrey."

"Yes, Mr. Varga?" "Could you bring in coffee for Mr. Rogers and me?"

"Certainly. Right away."

She didn't have to ask what we took in the coffee as she always came in with a plate of sugar, sweetener, milk, and cream.

I returned to my chair and spoke to my client like a police captain briefing my team. "Here's how it's going to go down. We will apply an effective tool used in Neuro Linguistic Pro-gramming (NLP) known as Time Line Therapy (TLT).

Significant events in your life cause your brain to search for comparable memories. Time Line Therapy magnifies the current event with a pleasant scenario or a frightening scenario that may unleash an array of unwarranted negative emotions. Twenty-five percent of the negative emotions are nonsense, and three-quarters are garbage, making it one hundred percent recyclable." Mr. Rogers laughed.

"We will be trashing all the negative emotions this morning. You'll be a new man."

"We're going to do that all-in-one session?"

"Of course," I said. "Why do you think I charge so much?"

"You're funny," he laughed.

My secretary opened the door with a tray of coffee, condiments, and cookies. She placed them on the table in front of the sofa. "Will there be anything else?"

"No, that's fine. Thanks so much. No calls or interruptions. TLT is about to commence."

"Very well then," she smiled and quickly turned for the door as if wanting to avoid the firing line of TLT. As we sipped our coffee and nibbled on cookies, I simplified the TLT method.

"In Time Line Therapy, you will visualize your life as a straight line stretched-out from birth to the present and beyond to the future. The line stretching from your right side represents the past, your left side represents the future, and your middle point represents the present. As you move along the right side of the line you re-experience past events. Imagine yourself floating safely above the time line—observing, not experiencing. As you move along the left side of the line into the future imagine how it feels to be free—note your accomplishments. As we interpret your experience you can release fear and other negative feelings. Place the negative feelings in a box where they can cause no further harm—you can talk about them and think about them, but they will not affect you.

I will guide you as you move along the time line and effectively help you deal with issues should they arise. My client took a deep breath.

"Cool. Let's do this!"

Session Two:

As I closed my office door at the end of the day, I was exhausted but felt a sense of satisfaction and accomplishment about the day's therapy sessions. I was surprised to see my secretary waiting for me. She appeared distraught and looked at me through tear filled eyes.

"Are you okay Audrey?"

"Trouble in paradise, she replied. I think my wife and I may be breaking up."

"Audrey, I don't work on weekends, but I'll make an exception. I will schedule a session for you and your wife on Saturday morning."

It can be difficult to leave a relationship when couples have been together for multiple years. Conflict and lack of intimacy are common in relationships. One partner may feel that working through conflicts could change the relationship for the better. One partner could exit the relationship at the meagre presence of a disagreement. One partner may engage in an extramarital affair, and their partner may reluctantly stay in the relationship hoping that the one cheating will see the light. A therapist can often reveal hidden hurts by simply redirecting or rephrasing a clients' expressed feelings.

Audrey and her wife Grace were in the office early Saturday morning. Coffee was brewing when I arrived, and they brought muffins. They looked happy, and in love, so I wondered what issues they were facing.

"Good morning Mr. Varga; thank you for seeing us on short notice and on a Saturday. Your wife must be a saint."

"She is, Audrey, she is. Both saint and sinner."

"This is my lovely wife Grace," Audrey said with her arm wrapped around Grace. Grace reached out a rigid hand, and I shook it.

"Nice to meet you, Grace. Thanks for the coffee and muffins," I said.

"You're welcome," they chimed together. I grabbed a warm muffin and a coffee.
"Shall we, ladies?" I said and motioned to my office door.

"We shall," Audrey responded.

They put their breakfast treats on the table and sat down. I did the same.

"So, what issue has come up in your marriage that you want to resolve today?"

Audrey began, "We don't have time for each other anymore. Grace is exhausted by the time she comes home from work. She wants to grab a drink, a joint, and chill on the sofa in front of the tv."

"Do you have favourite shows you watch together?"

"Oh yes, we enjoy watching a variety of sitcoms while holding hands on the couch," Audrey said.

"Nice to have something in common," I said. "Sure, is, but we watch tv for an hour and go to bed."

"Our time together consists of an hour before bed and an hour before work. Weekends are spent with LGBT festivities, shopping for groceries, stuff like that. Occasionally we make time to walk on the beach or visit a few botanical gardens," Audrey said.

"Do you spend more time together on weekends? Shopping and festivities count as time spent together," I said.

"Yes, that's true," Audrey replied.

"What other fun activities do you do together? Have you ever gone wine tasting?"

"Yes, that's what we're planning today after therapy."

"Same with my wife and I," I responded, then regretted it. Therapists rarely share personal information with their clients about themselves and their activities.

"Maybe we'll see you both later," Grace flirted.

"See, that's one of Grace's behaviours that I find hurtful," Audrey exclaimed.

"She flirts with other people, and I'm uncomfortable when she touches others."

Audrey and her wife, Grace, are a unique couple. Grace's chosen profession prompts Audrey to feel emotionally cheated.

"Tell me more about the flirting," I said.

"Many weekends, Grace is invited to parties and conferences and flirts to gain new clients."

"How would you know? You're not there with me," Grace replied.

"I know," Audrey said.

"Is this true, Grace?" I spoke.

"Sure, it's true. It's done all the time in my profession; get clients hooked," Grace said.

"Except you aren't a hooker," Audrey added.

"Correct," Grace said matter of fact.

"I give discounts to fellow therapists if you're interested, Albert."

Albert? Did she just call me Albert?

"It's Mr. Varga," Audrey said, fuming.

"Audrey is right, Grace, and I'm not interested in playing with anyone but my wife; I'm a licensed, therapist."

"And you're just a girl who gets paid for turning on rich executives so they can go home to their wives and satisfy them," Audrey interjected.

"I don't see you complaining about the money. Why are you working here anyway? I can support both of us lavishly," Grace replied.

"I just like to have an income and a respectable job," said Audrey.

That took her off guard, and it looked like she was considering what Audrey had said.

Grace replied, "You knew what I did for a living, and you accepted it right from the start. Look, I only make love to you, never with my clients. As I said, it's illegal to do so anyway. I run a respectable business."

"What is it you do, Grace? Are you a couple's counsellor? Do couples come to you for intervention?"

"Rarely. But look, here's what it's all about." Grace was very thorough and surprisingly professional, like she was reading from her dissertation thesis. Audrey looked fearful and guilty, but guilty of what?

"Audrey, Grace, I understand the relationship was at a point where you both were going to break," I said.

"True. So?" they both chimed.

"Was there an understanding that you were free to see others?"

"Well, we were officially on a break, so I guess we were free to see other people. But I only love Audrey. Male or female, it doesn't matter. I only love Audrey. I knew we could work things out, and we would be back with each other," Grace replied.

Audrey went pale. I know that look; I've seen it in other couples.

"So, Grace, you are saying you were free to see others during the break, but you chose not to see anybody. Is that correct?" I asked.

"You, sir, are correct," Grace replied.

"Are you sure, Grace?" I asked.

"Well, um," she said to her shoes.

"Well, what?" Audrey prompted.

"I'm sorry, Audrey, it meant nothing, just consensual sex. Not with a client but with this guy I met as I was walking alone on the beach," Grace replied. Audrey was visibly shaken.

"Is there something you want to share, Audrey?" I prompted.

"I forgive you," Audrey said.
"No reason to forgive me; we were on a break. All bets were off," Grace replied.

"Anything else you'd like to share, Audrey?"

Audrey breathed a sigh of relief. "I cheated on you too."

Grace appeared shocked and hurt. Odd for someone who cheated as well.

"So, what are you girls feeling? Are you calling it even and moving on?" I asked. "They both looked at me, shocked. "I mean moving on from what happened and having a fresh start with each other and open and honest communication?" They looked at each other, then at me then at each other. They cried, hugged, and then looked at me as if to say thank you, but were speechless.

"Thank you." they both chimed.

"Sweetie, look, I love you. I don't want to see you hurt. We can work this out. I can cut my hours after my book deal comes out this fall. You can come on tour with me. We will have plenty of time together," Grace said.

Audrey looked up at me as if she asked permission to leave her job to go on tour. She didn't have to ask.

"It's up to you." I shrugged. "I'm good."

Grace looked at me.

"I'm working on a movie deal for my book." Audrey perked up.

"Really, why didn't you tell me?" Audrey asked.

"It's still in progress, not guaranteed. I'll insist the producers give you a part in the movie. A respectable role." Grace tenderly kissed her wife and held her close.

"I love you, Audrey."

"I love you, Grace."

"That's a wrap, ladies." I spoke.

They smiled and got up.

"Thanks for everything Alb…I mean Mr. Varga."

"No problem. I'll give the bill to Audrey, Monday when she comes to work." I spoke.

"Yes, that's cool. The book tour won't be for a while yet. I'll let you have plenty of notice," Grace said.

The perfect ending.

Many people feel depressed at one time or another. We can choose to dwell on the feelings and listen to the negative inner voice that tells us there is no answer, or we can listen to the cheerful inner voice that tells us there is a way out of our negative emotional state. Most people think it's impossible to take positive action when in a rut, but it's pretty simple.

1. Examine your negative feelings and depressed thoughts.

2. Create a plan of action and follow up with it.

3. Write down your thoughts and feelings in a book. Read them and ask yourself, are things that bad? How can I avoid these false feelings and patterns of behaviour?

4. Exercise. Walk, swim, bike, lift light weights. Punch a punching bag. Exercise is good for you, makes you happy, and clears your thinking.

5. Talk with a trustworthy friend.

6. Help someone else by getting involved in your community. It feels good to help others.

7. Take a break from the mundane and go to a movie, have a bath, watch a funny video.

8. All the above suggestions will lift you out of your negative slump.

Session Three:

I arrived at the office on Monday morning, my client was early and chatting with Audrey. I introduced myself and ushered him into my office. He turned and thanked Audrey for the coffee.

"Nice secretary, you got there," he said as he closed the office door.

"She's efficient, polite, and friendly," I responded like it was no big deal.

"Very pretty too," he responded.

"So, Paul, what area of your life will you be changing this morning," I said.

"I am a manic depressive and unemployed because of my disability. My wife works full time, and occasionally puts me down or teases me about my condition. I struggle with low self-esteem, periods of depression with thoughts of suicide, and I make mountains out of molehills when it comes to my negative emotions," Paul said.

"Sounds like you may be feeding your brain data that reinforces your negative emotions. I will explain what I mean later. Let's talk about your bouts of depression first," I said. "Do you know why you feel depressed? Can you describe your physical sensations when experiencing depression? "

"I feel exhausted, tired, crying, worn out," Paul said. "

What specifically were you depressed about the last time?"

"I felt suicidal and depressed about pretty much every-thing over the last few weeks, especially the wedding," he said.

"Can you break that down? What specifically depressed you or bothered you about the wedding?"

"What bothered me were my brothers and how they treat me."

"Can you be more specific? Provide one example of how your brothers treated you," I asked.

"It's like I have no purpose; I asked my older brother if he wanted to spend time with me, he said no."

"Okay, so you felt down about that, right?"

"Yes, it's like I have no one on my side; I felt alone," he said.

"What I'd like you to do is look at the following list of cognitive distortions. They are taken from the book, 'Felling Better' by Dr. David D Burns."

1. All or nothing thinking: You see things in black and white categories. If your performance falls short of perfect, you are seeing yourself as a total failure.

2. Over-generalization: You see a single adverse event as a never-ending pattern of defeat.

3. Mental filter: You can pick out a single negative detail and dwell on it exclusively so that your vision of all reality becomes darkened, like the drop of ink that discolours the entire beaker of water.

4. Disqualifying the positive: You reject positive experiences by insisting they don't count for some reason or another. In this way you can maintain a negative belief contradicted by your everyday experiences.

5. Jumping to conclusions: You make a negative interpretation even though there are no definite facts that convincingly support your conclusion.

    a. Mind-reading: You arbitrarily conclude that some-one is negatively reacting to you, and you don't bother to check this out.

    b. The fortune-teller error: You anticipate that things will turn out badly, and you feel convinced that your prediction is already a fact.

6. Magnification: You exaggerate the importance of things, or you inappropriately shrink things until they appear tiny (your desirable qualities).

7. Emotional reasoning: You assume that your negative emotions necessarily reflect how things are: 'I feel it; therefore, it must be true.'

8. Should statements: You try to motivate yourself with should and shouldn't as if you have to be whipped and punished before you can expect to do anything. "Musts" and "ought" to be also offenders. The emotional conse-quence is guilt. When you direct should-statements to-ward others, you feel anger, frustration, and resentment.

9. Labeling and Mis-labeling: Instead of describing your error, you attach a negative label to yourself: "I'm a loser."

10. Personalization: You see yourself as the cause of some adverse external event for which you are not primarily responsible.

11. Moving forward, when you are depressed or feeling sad, get a piece of paper and draw three equal columns. In the first column write what is causing your feelings of sadness or depression. In the second column write the cognitive distortion that applies to your situation. In the third column write a positive statement. "Do you follow so far?"

"Yes, I do."

"Let's use the example of your brother not wanting to see you. Enter this situation in column one. In column two, look up the generalizations and apply them to your brother not wanting to see you. What generalization would apply to the situation?" "I am not sure," Paul replied.

"How did you feel about your brother not wanting to see you?"

"I feel like I am nothing, and I have nothing to offer," he said.

"Okay, how about jumping to conclusions or labelling?"

"In the third column, you could write—I have a lot to offer, just not to him. Perhaps he has no time for me because of other priorities."

"I appreciate this, but I am not sure I can do it," Paul replied.

"What do you feel you can't do specifically?"

"I get depressed, and nothing works," he said.

"Now look carefully at the cognitive distortions: all or nothing thinking, over generalization, and mental filter. What best applies to that statement?"

"All three apply," he said. "You have the right idea," I said. "In the third column you could write, I am only basing this on past mistakes. I will start slowly and see positive results." "Sounds good, eh? "

"Yes," Paul replied.

"This requires daily homework. If you are not depressed on a particular day, recall a past depression and apply the principles." "You must recondition your mind. "

"Now let's talk about your self-esteem! That's a biggie, eh?"

"Yes, impossible. That will never change."

"Essentially, you identify as a house husband with no job and a few social contacts, right?"

"Right."

"Go back to the list of cognitive distortions and apply the appropriate distortion. You said, your self-esteem is impossible, and that it will never change."

"I feel like jumping to conclusions would be an appropriate choice."

"I agree. Not many people catch on this quickly. You have a sharp analytical mind."

"Can you describe a typical day?"

"I get up and go to the library. I am out of the house from 9:00 am until 2:00 pm."

"What happens when you return home?"
"Not much, sometimes I nap, do laundry, or talk on the chat lines."

"My wife never says much about what I do, occasionally she speaks negatively about my lifestyle. Guess she's making the bucks.

"Sometimes her teasing is hurtful."
"What does she tease you about?"

"How I look, my art, etc."

"Tell me about how you look?"

"I am fat and ugly."

"Now tell me what YOU see when you look in the mirror."

"I see a fat, ugly guy."

"How does she tease you about your looks?"

"She says I'm a wide load; she calls me fat butt. She tells me not to wear certain clothes."

"You told me earlier you two have a great romantic life. Does she get turned on by fat ugly men? What does she look like?"

"She has long blonde hair, green eyes, a slim build, and very attractive."

"Do you have many friends?"

"A few."

"Does she ever tell you she loves you?"

"Yes."

"How does that make you feel?"

"I just think she says it but doesn't mean it. She is constantly teasing me."

"What cognitive distortion reflects your statement, she says she loves you, but you don't believe her?"

"Number four, disqualifying the positive, right?" "Excellent!!! For now, I'm afraid our time is up, but stay with the daily homework Paul, and you'll start to feel better. I believe you already feel better."

"Okay, and yes, I do, thank you."

I thought the session with Paul was productive until I got a follow-up call from him begging for another appointment.

"Hey, Paul. Have a seat."

"How are you?"

Paul began. "I am fine, how are you?

How was your weekend?"

"Saturday night was terrible, dreadful. I find out that my levels were deficient."

"Paul, your levels will stabilize, and you will feel better. "

"Last night, I was feeling suicidal. I tried to practice cognitive distortions but they're not working, nothing is."

"Are you feeling suicidal now?"

"I have my moments. I have to be honest I want the pain to end; I have had enough. The only way to end it all is to over-dose. No bloody messes. I know how much medication to take."

"Paul are you able to recognize any blessings about your lifestyle?"

"No, not really. On the outside I appear fabulous, but my inner emotional state is not so good."

"Paul are you able to change the internal dialogue—I am experiencing random misfiring's, and I don't want to kill my-self. I want to live fully alive."

"That is a beautiful thought but sometimes I don't think that quickly. I get stuck. I just had this conversation with my wife, she told me to get over it."

"Is it possible you just need to practice?"
"I don't care anymore."

"Paul, I don't care anymore is a random misfire!"

"You have an answer for everything. I don't know, some-times I just don't know. I just don't want to keep going anymore."

"Another misfiring. Paul, if I had a nickel for every one of my misfiring's, I'd have $3.65."

Paul was not responding to my humour. "This is the worst I have felt in a long time."

"Hmm, let's see that's 65 cents for you so far. Catching on?"

"I guess."

"Write down your thoughts and assign a nickel to every negative   random misfiring. Everything   negative is a random misfiring. Do you believe that?"

"I believe it's possible that you don't believe me. How I feel. You doubt it all."

"I am trying to teach you how to recognize that your thoughts do not define you."

"Paul, do you have a red jacket?"

"No, I have a white jacket."

"When you put on the white jacket are you a part of it?"

"Yes."

"You are in the sense that you feel the comfort and warmth, correct?"

"Yes."

"Can you take the jacket off at will?"

"Yes."

"So, the jacket is not composed of the same molecules as you."

"No, it is not."

"In the same sense, your essence is detached from your thoughts and feelings. You feel hot, and your thoughts prompt you to take the jacket off."

"You can't stop random thoughts from misfiring's—just like you can't stop a bird from flying overhead and dropping feces, right?"

"Right."

"You can; however, stop the bird from growing a nest on your head, right?"

"Yes."

"The feelings are like the bird who has dropped feces, you can brush it away, but it will come back. Through proper therapy, adjustment, and practice, thoughts will come back but won't take up residence; they will just fly overhead."

"Imagine that I offered you a beautiful dinner and after we ate, I told you it was poisonous. I advised you that you had a half-hour to live but I had the antidote—would you believe me?"

"Even if I stated I was joking, I challenge that you may begin to catastrophize your thought life, and you may experience difficulty breathing. Your mind may attempt to convince you that your body was sick and dying."

"Yes, you are right. I can see that."

"Similarly, with mental illness, your mind can convince you that you are chronically ill and dying after self-diagnosing symptoms via a Dr. Google consultation.

"So, what is your advice?"

"Brush the negative thoughts away and take off the jacket."

"Okay. I will try. I am just not sure I can do it because I am so tired."

"Regardless of how tired you are, don't give up—things will get better."

"I will focus on something else—something cheerful."

"Right. There you go. Take your mind off it." I ushered him out of the office and was confident he would be fine.

As it turned out, Paul's condition greatly improved as the result of a combination of medication and psychotherapy from his psychiatrist. In his case, stress management and NLP were only a Band-Aid solution until he could undergo a medical assessment from his doctor.

Session Four:

I greeted Jane with my usual ear-to-ear smile.

"Hi," she replied as if it were an inconvenience to respond. She immediately took a seat on the office couch.

"What can I do for you this fine day," I said.

"My relationship," she said.

Well, at least she is getting straight to the point.

"What about your relationship?"

"Well, my husband is usually in a bad mood."

"Usually?"

"Yes, he's a good father, treats the kids like gold."

"And you?"

"He treats me like dirt," she responded.

"How so?"

"He thinks I'm his slave," she said.

"Do you work?"

"No, he supports us. He has a good job. I take care of the kids. He expects me to clean the house, cook daily meals, and bathe him."

"How long has this been going on? Are you a slave or a homemaker? Besides the hot baths, I know a lot of happy relationships where   the   wife is the homemaker and the husband the breadwinner."

"Yeah, I guess. Well, there's more," she said.

"I thought there might be," I said, leaning forward in my chair.

"Well, he forces sex on me."

"Spousal rape?"

"Yes,"

"Does he think it is his right to have sex with you at will?"

"Yes."

"Do you love him?"

"I don't know."

"Have you told him how you feel?"

"Once, he just smiled, shrugged his shoulders, and walked out of the room."

"Does your husband have other behaviours that upset you?"

"Yes, sometimes he yells when he gets drunk, I just stay out of his way. My dad used to yell when he got drunk."

"Are you afraid of your husband?"

"No, not if I do as I'm told. He's quite pleasant when he isn't drinking."

"So, he treats you like a sex slave, but there are rewards or good times?"

"Sure, he takes me and the kids out, but I can't put up with sex on demand!"

"What would happen if you refused him?"

"I don't want to think about it. He'd kill me probably. What can I do?"

"There are organizations, women's shelters, and victims' services that help women who report cases of domestic violence."

"Victims services, I've heard of them."

"Would you like to connect with one of these organizations?"

"No, I am scared. What if he beats me? What if he takes the kids?"

"What about calling to learn about potential options and resources?"

"Okay, I'll call tomorrow."

"Do you have any place to go? Do you have friends you can stay with?"

"My aunt offered the kids and me a room."

"Are you willing to take the kids, go to your aunt's and leave your husband a note?"

"Okay."

"Tell your husband you don't like being forced into sex and that if he wants the relationship to continue, he has to attend counselling with you."

"Okay, I'll think about it."

"Jane, our time is up. Here is a list of contact numbers for local crisis services and resources for women fleeing domestic violence."

I received a phone call from Jane one week later. She reported that he forced sex on her one last time. After weighing the pros and cons of their relationship she decided to go to her aunt's and called victims' services. Jane reported that her husband agreed to attend counselling and they are working on their marriage.

Session Five:

My next client arrived on time. He walked into my office with his head tilted downward.

"How are you feeling today?" I greeted with a smile.

"How am I doing?" he responded as if to say, isn't it obvious?

"Yes," I said cautiously. He smiled ever so slightly. His lips started to quiver, and he started weeping. "I'm afraid of dying."

"How long have you known you were dying?" "He looked up at me as if he had just had a revelation.

"No, no, don't misunderstand. I'm not dying. I'm just afraid of dying."

"I think we all are, but the real cause of death is being born. We can't avoid death; the trick is not to think about it and enjoy life. Worry robs us of our happiness."

"Yeah, but when I die, I'm going to Hell." "Why do you say that?"

"I'm a born-again Christian, and I'm going to Hell."

"Why, as a Christian, do you feel you're going to Hell?"

"I was in a charismatic cult in high school, and they said if I left the group, I would die, and Satan would come and get me."

"It's been a while since high school; do you still believe you're going to hell?"

"Yes, because I'm a purposeful sinner and for purposeful sinners there is no sacrifice."

Hebrews 10:26 NIV

If we deliberately keep on sinning after we have received the knowledge of the truth, no sacrifice for sins is left.

"Is it possible this passage was taken out of context? Could the scripture be referring to unbelievers who purposely and continually denied who Christ was? Is it possible there was no forgiveness because they choose not to accept Jesus' forgiveness?"

He leaned back on the sofa and smiled, "I never thought of it that way."

"Of course, cults rarely allow their members to think for themselves."

His head nodded, "Please do go on."

"God loves you. He will not abandon you. You are the apple of His eye.

Here are a few scriptures to help you discover your identity in Christ.

1. "Very truly I tell you, whoever hears my word and believes him who sent me has eternal life and will not be judged but has crossed over from death to life." John 5:24 NIV

2. "All those the Father gives me will come to me, and whoever comes to me I will never drive away." John 6:37 NIV

3. "I give them eternal life, and they shall never perish; no one will snatch them out of my hand." John 10:28 NIV

4. "I am the vine (Jesus); you are the branches. If you remain in me and I in you, you will bear much fruit; apart from me you can do nothing." John 15:5 NIV

5. "And everyone who calls on the name of the Lord will be saved." Acts 2:21 NIV

6. "All the prophets testify about him that everyone who believes in him receives forgiveness of sins through his name." Acts 10:43 NIV

7. "Blessed is the one whose sin the Lord will never count against them." Romans 4:8 NIV

8. "Therefore, there is now no condemnation for those who are in Christ Jesus." Romans 8:1 NIV

9. "And that is what some of you were. But you were washed, you were sanctified, you were justified in the name of the Lord Jesus Christ and by the Spirit of our God." 1 Corinthians 6:11 NIV

10. "…that God was reconciling the world to himself in Christ, not counting people's sins against them. And he has committed to us the message of reconciliation." 2 Corinthians 5:19 NIV

"So, I can do what I want?" "Consider this, if you ate six pounds of chicken wings and a litre of soda all in one sitting, is it possible you would experience an upset stomach and a headache?" "Yes, it's possible," he responded.

"Did God punish you, or did you experience the consequences of your choice?" "You're funny," he laughed. He stood up, shook my hand, and left the office with an ear-to-ear smile.

In my practice, I deal with individuals who experience anxiety, panic attacks and obsessive-compulsive behaviour.

1. Anxiety attack can be defined as tension and anxiety over various situations.

2. Panic attack can be defined as episodes of anxiety and terror; feelings of intense fear or discomfort accompanied with physical symptoms such as: rapid heartbeat, sweats, shakes, shortness of breath, choking sensation, dizziness, nausea, numbness, hot flashes or chills, chest pain, fear of dying, and fear of going insane.

3. Obsessive-compulsive disorder can be defined as consistent mental images, thoughts, or ideas, resulting in compulsive behaviours such as repetitive routines intended to

ease the victim's comfort in some mystical way. Although individuals recognize that the obsessive thoughts and ritualized behaviour patterns are senseless and excessive, they cannot stop them.

Session Six:

aude walked into my office without an appointment and in a panic. She started crying.

"I don't know what's wrong with me. I don't know what to do. No one will help me. I don't have money."

"What brings you here today?

"I'm not doing good."

"What do you feel? "

"I feel like I can't breathe."

"Do you realize that you are breathing otherwise, you wouldn't be able to talk to me?"

"Yeah, I've got to calm down."

"That's right; I want you to take a deep breath in through your nose then blow it out gently through your mouth."

"Okay, I did."

"Good. Now do it again." She does. "Good. And one last time."

"Is that all I have to do, and I'm, okay?"

"I'm afraid it's not that simple, but it's a start. We'll take it one step at a time. Okay?"

"So, tell me, when do you usually experience these attacks?"

"In the car. I have to pull over to the side of the road and calm down."

"Do you always take the same route to and from work?"

"Yes, I usually experience attacks while driving on country roads."

"Funny, it is relaxing scenery, and oh God, no." She had another attack right in my office.

"What's wrong?"

"Um, I'm feeling another attack."

"Okay, just relax and take a deep breath. Think of something pleasant."

"No, I can't. I think I'm going to die! Ah! I have to call 911!"

"Listen to my voice. It's okay. Take a deep breath in through your nose and blow it out gently through your mouth."

"Okay, ah, I'm okay, but I'm shaking."

"Yes, I see that. That's okay, that's normal. I'd be worried if you didn't shake. It'll stop soon."

"Okay, yeah, deep breath. Okay"
"What colour is your car?" I ask her.

"Blue"

"Is blue your favourite colour?"

"Yes."

"Where do you live?"

"In a house."

"Are you attempting to divert my attention?"

"For now, yes, but there are a lot of underlying issues in your life you have to resolve. The trick is not to dwell on your past but learn from the specifics and forget the details." "Okay, thanks," she said and got up to leave.

"Woe there, we're not done yet. We've got to figure out what is causing these attacks."

Over the many subsequent sessions, I thought it would be in her best interests to consult with a psychologist who specialized in childhood traumas.

As it turns out, when she was five years old, her dad often took her out for rides in the country to see the horses and other natural resources. Sometimes he would take his eye off the road and nearly drive into a ditch. After alerting her father to his mistake, he would slap her across the face, throw her out of the car, and drive away. She was terrified, not knowing where she was. Her dad would return 30 minutes later to pick her up and ask her if she had learned her lesson.

She came to realize that every time she drove through the country, her unconscious would trigger the memory of the event, triggering the panic attack.

Session Seven:

Debra was right on time for her first appointment. Audrey ushered her into my office while I was still sipping coffee at my desk. Audrey motioned her to the couch and said, "Make yourself comfortable. May I offer you some fresh coffee?"

Debra was surprised, "Yes, please. I'm getting the royal treatment."

"We do our best to make our clients happy and comfortable."

Audrey returned in under five minutes with a tray of coffee, cream, sugar, sweetener, milk, and chocolate chip cookies.

"So, what brings you here besides your car?" I began with some droll humour. She smirked but was otherwise occupied in thought.

"Well, that's just it; it's all about the car. I am afraid of driving and having panic attacks."

"Tell me more about the fear you experience when driving."

"I am so scared to get in the car and drive more than I have to."

"Okay, so you'll drive to places for your immediate needs, survival, or necessity but will not take any pleasure trips. What stops you? What do you feel will happen if you venture to the mall?"

"I get violent and very belligerent, like I'd rather wreck the car than drive someplace."

"Is your fear with the driving, or going to the mall? In other words, would you have the same reaction if you took a bus to the mall?"

"No, just driving to the mall. I'm learning to love the bus."

"So, this has occurred before then. What exactly happened, and how far did you get with the drive?"

"I walked to the parking lot to get my car and began getting very upset, felt like I was going to wreck the car and kill myself and others if I drove. That sounds dumb, doesn't it? The only way I get to school is by turning my radio up loud." "That isn't dumb. Quite logical. What you are experiencing is a temporary chemical imbalance caused by an unconscious reminder of a past event." "Tell me about a past driving event."

"I have been driving since the age of 21. I passed the driver's education program and was encouraged to schedule my driving test. My ex attempted to discourage me through put downs, scary driving tales, and screaming at minor driving mistakes."

"Finally, I got my license. He insisted I drive with him once to prove my skill set, but after driving with him for three months I couldn't stand to have him in the car with me. I was afraid to go anywhere in case I made mistakes."

"Is it fair to say that you could only get to school by yelling, cursing, and having the radio up—symbolically drowning out your ex's gobbledy-gook!"

"Yes!"

"Are you open to a visualization exercise?"

"Okay."

"Visualize yourself in a movie theatre. You are viewing a movie of yourself driving a car on a pleasurable vacation. Let me know when you have turned on the ignition."

"Okay, I'm in the car and have turned on the ignition."

"Now, visualize your ex sitting in the passenger seat. What is he saying?"

"Okay, I can see him. He says this is a new car, don't wreck it."

"How will you respond to him?"

"I ask him if he thinks I intentionally intend on wrecking the car."

"Now, what does he say?"

"He tells me to give him the keys because I am not responsible enough to drive the car."

"I tell him the car is mine not his!"

"How does he respond?"

"He grabs the keys from the ignition and gets out of the car."

I yell, "NO! This is my car!"

"Good, now visualize yourself walking up to him and yanking the keys from his hand. You look across the road and notice a biker is watching to see that you are not hurt. What happens now?"

"I get in the car, drive to school and park the car."

"Awesome! Your ex is left in awe. He can't figure out why he has no control. The biker laughs, he's going to tell his buddies about the whole situation."

"Your mind is a collection of movies that project images, generally negative images which are exaggerated and not accurate. This technique can help you replace fear.

Go to the movie theatre in your mind and create a positive movie; if a scene comes up while you're driving, just think of the biker escorting you and your ex.

And remember that blasting the radio works as a distraction because your brain can only focus on one thing at a time while scanning six others."

Further sessions were conducted with success.

Session Eight:

My next appointment presented a bit of a challenge. Margie arrived 10 minutes ahead of schedule. Audrey ushered Margie in to take a seat on the couch and I sat in my therapist's chair.

"I'll be right in with coffee and cookies," Audrey said.

"So, what are the things we are going to change today, Margie?"

"I need to stop listening to the voices in my head. I need to stop recalling the images of the cult my parents forced me into."

"Sure, we can work on that," I said as if she requested extra chocolate sauce on her ice cream. As Margie munchied on cookies and sipped her coffee, I briefed her on the tools we were going to use in the session.

"So, based on what I've briefed you on, are you ready to begin?"

"Oh yes."

"Sweet. Now let's start with the voices in your head. Your parents, yes?"

"Yes"

"Are you willing to look at this from a different perspective?"

"Yes."

"Is it possible that your parents loved you but were mesmerized by the cult and unaware of how their involvement in the cult affected you?"

"Yes, it's possible."

"Great, are you willing to try the visualization technique I briefed you about earlier?"

"Sure."

"Okay, imagine yourself at home with your parents. You are sitting outside with them on the patio. Imagine the sun creating sparkles on top of the pool. Do you feel safe and relaxed in this place?"

"Yes."

"Now imagine yourself in the conservation with your parents. Imagine you are floating far above the situation.

Observe their mannerisms, their hand gestures, their head movements. Now imagine yourself catching a laser gun that I throw at you."

"Got it."

"Nice catch."

"Thanks."

"You caught it like a pro."

"Be aware that your parents are only an image of the past; they cannot be harmed. Zap them with the laser gun, and they will disappear. They will no longer be able to harass your thoughts."

She raised the laser gun, zap, bull's eye, they disintegrated, or at least that's what she imagined.

"That was fun," she said, opening her eyes after counting from ten to one. Did I perform hypnosis on her? Not at all. Hypnosis is far different and should only be practiced under the care of a physician.

Another rapid tool to use when you are stressed or have unrealistic images in your mind is called the white-out method.

"So, like splash white-out liquid over the image, and it disappears?" "No, but if that process works for you, use it."

"I am referring to making the image brighter and brighter until it whites out. If the image comes back later, repeat the method." "Got it. It makes a lot of sense."

Next, I engaged Margie in an exercise that would help her change negative thinking patterns.

"Margie, I want to encourage you to flood your brain daily with positive, relaxing images. Imagine yourself getting a Swedish massage. Feel the endorphins flooding your body."

"Okay."

"Now form a circle with your right thumb and index finger. As you go about your day you can form that circle any time you feel stressed, and you will feel a similar endorphin rush throughout your body."

"This process will vanish any negative, fearful images that may appear in your consciousness. Do this three-times a day or more if you like."

"Sweet."

"Yes, sweet," I laughed.

Session Nine:

My next appointment was with Dana, who suffered from obsessive-compulsive disorder and anxiety. When you have an anxiety or panic attack, a simple, quick, and efficient way to deescalate is:

1. Breathe in for four seconds.

2. Hold your breath for six seconds.

3. Exhale your breath for eight seconds,

4. Repeat once or twice until relief comes.

5. This causes the autonomic nervous system to shift from a sympathetic state to a parasympathetic response.

"What's on your mind that you'd like to change today, Dana? "

"Oh, there's something wrong with me. The doctor says its anxiety attacks. Sometimes I feel like I can't breathe."

"Sounds like you're doing the right thing by consulting a doctor. What do you think triggers the attacks?"

"I get flashbacks of getting beat up by my father; then I can't breathe. He always said he was going to kill me. At his funeral I stood by his coffin, and I couldn't cry. My brother snuck up behind me and frightened me! I was startled and fainted over my father's body. The event is in the past, but I can't get rid of the visual."

"Tell me one thing you like; a favourite colour, smell, sight, or sound."

"I like my girlfriend."

"Okay, good. You like your girlfriend."

"Yes, it calms me down when I look at her picture and smell her perfume. I keep a photo of her in my wallet."

"How did you meet her? Where was the picture taken?" "We met at a bus stop. Our favourite song is, Bus Stop by the Hollys." "Hey, I'm starting to feel better!"

"You feel better because your mind is focused on love and pleasant thoughts, versus negative."

"The next time you feel the onset of an attack, remember how much love you feel at this moment. Tell yourself that you are going to be all right. Do you think you can try that?"

"Absolutely."

"How can I manage obsessive-compulsive behaviour? "

"Like what, for example? "

"I'm constantly washing my hands for fear of contamination."

"Your doctor is the best person to talk to for that because sometimes that behaviour is chemically induced. But I can give you a quick panacea to help you manage the behaviour until you make an appointment."

"I'm listening."

1. Relabel: Recognize the fact that the intrusive thought and urge is the result of a random misfiring in the brain brought about through habitual negative thinking

2. Reattribute: Realize that a random misfiring causes the intensity and intrusiveness of the thought/urge in the brain brought about through habitual negative thinking

3. Refocus: Workaround the negative thoughts but focus your attention on something else, or at least for a few minutes--do another behaviour

4. Revalue: Do not take the intrusive thought at face value. It is not significant in itself. It is not meaningful, and there is no evidence to back up the thought.

"These are excerpts from the book Brain Lock."

"Thanks, these tools will be helpful."

"Great, well, it seems like our time is up for today. Let me know how things are going, and we will see if you need another session."

Conclusion

In conclusion, remember that:

1. Imagery is compelling for achieving your goals. Imagine your dreams as if you've already achieved them.

2. Learn to discern stress and recognize associated triggers. This way, you can 'nip them in the bud.'

3. Applaud your life.

4. Lighten up, take the seriousness out of situations.

5. Laugh, hug, tickle.

6. Have a day of psychodrama with your mate. You are king for a day; she is queen for a day. Your imagination only limits you!

7. Don't Worry—Get Happy!

8. Finally, heed the words of my long-time friend who, after he had a bit too much to drink, I asked him how he handles stress."

He said, "That's easy dude, you just don't…um…don't."

I said, "Yes?"

He replied, "It's just that you um…sorry, what was the question?

I said, "How do you handle stress?"

He said, "Well um…you, kind of like um…sorry man, I forgot what I was going to say."

I said, "I wanted to know how you handle stress."

He said, "Ah, come on man, just forget about it!"

I replied, "You, sir, are correct!"